FIND YOUR OWN
FUNDAMENTALS

GOLF DIGEST LEARNING LIBRARY
VOLUME 2

FIND YOUR OWN FUNDAMENTALS

Develop a full swing routine in five easy steps and start playing with your best shots consistently.

BOB TOSKI and JIM FLICK
with Larry Dennis

illustrations by Elmer Wexler

POCKET BOOKS
New York   London   Toronto   Sydney   Tokyo   Singapore

Published by:

Golf Digest/Tennis, Inc.
A New York Times Company,
5520 Park Avenue, Box 395
Trumbull, CT 06611-0395

and

POCKET BOOKS, a division of Simon & Schuster Inc.
1230 Avenue of the Americas
New York, NY 10020

Illustrations by Elmer Wexler

Book Design by Laura Hough

ISBN: 0-671-75870-5

First Golf Digest/Tennis, Inc. and Pocket Books
trade paperback printing July 1992

10 9 8 7 6 5 4 3 2 1

POCKET and colophon are registered trademarks
of Simon & Schuster Inc.

GOLF DIGEST/TENNIS, INC. and logo are trademarks of
Golf Digest/Tennis, Inc., A New York Times Company

Printed in the U.S.A.

CONTENTS

FIND YOUR OWN FUNDAMENTALS

1

FUNDAMENTALS—THE IMPORTANT FIRST STEP

There is more than one way to swing a golf club effectively. Jack Nicklaus swings it differently than Lee Trevino, whose swing is different than Gary Player's. Arnold Palmer has his unique style. Hale Irwin, Tom Kite and Curtis Strange don't swing alike. Yet all are great champions.

What each of these and other fine players have in common are solid pre-shot fundamentals. These fundamentals may vary with the individual, but each player has developed a set that works for him.

Most amateurs who come to us for lessons want us to work on their swings. They are not satisfied with the way they are striking the ball, so they obviously think the problem lies in the way they are swinging at it.

On the other hand, almost all the Tour professionals who we see want us first to check their setup—their posture, body alignment and clubface aim. They understand all too

Sam Snead, Tom Watson, Lee Trevino and Jack Nicklaus all swing differently ....but effectively.

well a principle that most amateurs either don't appreciate or ignore—your setup dictates the way you swing the club, and your swing can only be as consistent as that setup.

The good, experienced player recognizes that if his swing isn't working properly, it's probably because his setup isn't allowing it to work. He knows that if he gets his pre-shot fundamentals back in working order, his swing once again will begin to function well and consistently.

Good golfers prepare for success, and they do so by developing the pre-shot fundamentals that relate to the way they want to swing the golf club. Poor golfers prepare for disaster, usually by paying little attention to those important steps that must occur before the swing begins.

You need only two things to strike a golf ball—some kind of setup and some kind of swing motion. To strike the ball well and consistently on line, the setup and the motion must be compatible with each other and with the target.

The setup is the most important element in a successful—or unsuccessful—swing. So when you are having trouble, check that first. You almost always will find the answer to your problems, which occur because your swing instinctively will accommodate itself to your posture, aim and alignment. In other words, no matter how you stand to the ball and no matter where you aim, you will make a swing that will try to get the ball to the target. If your set-up and aim are correct, everything will be fine. If they are not, you're going to make compensations or adjustments in your swing, and therein lies danger.

* * *

Let's take a moment to examine the ball-flight laws or influences. Understanding them will let you understand why the ball goes where it does and is the first step in learning to set up and swing correctly. There are only four elements in a golf shot—distance, trajectory, starting direction and curve. The five factors that create those characteristics are:

1. Clubhead path at impact.
2. Clubface position at impact.
3. Squareness of contact.
4. Angle of approach.
5. Clubhead speed.

These are the things that determine the flight of the ball—why a ball slices or hooks, goes high or low and travels far or not so far.

Discounting trajectory and distance, there are only nine ways a golf ball can travel. It can start on a line to the left of the target and from there can continue straight, curve farther left or curve to the right. It can start straight at the target, continue straight or curve left or right. It can start to the right of the target and keep going straight or curve left or right. Obviously, the variations within those nine basic flight patterns are limitless.

The theoretically perfect swing would have you arriving at impact with the clubhead traveling on a path to the

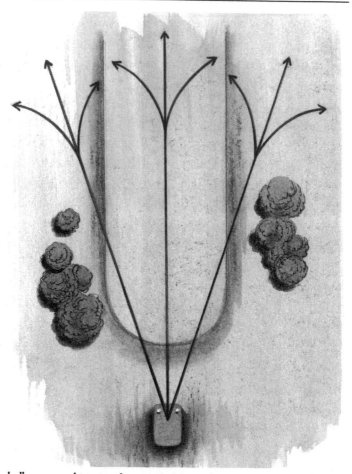

The ball can travel in nine directions, starting left, straight or right and either staying straight or curving left or right from those starting paths.

target line, at the proper angle in relation to the ground and with sufficient speed, the clubface aiming directly down the target line and contacting the ball squarely on the sweet spot. The ball then will travel straight down your target line with the proper trajectory and will go the distance you intended. Recognizing and correcting the deviations from that perfection makes a knowledge of the ball-flight laws vital to your success.

The two factors that determine the initial direction of the ball and, to a great extent, how it curves are *clubhead path* and *clubface position*. Their effects are interrelated. For example, if your clubhead at impact is traveling directly toward your target but your clubface is open, the ball will start somewhat in the direction of the target but will slice or curve to the right. If the clubface is closed, the ball will start reasonably straight and then will hook or curve to the left.

If your clubhead path is from outside to inside the target line—traveling to the left of your target—and your clubface is square to that line, the ball will start left and fly straight on that line. If your clubface is open, the ball will start left and curve to the right. If it is closed, the ball will start left and curve to the left. The opposite is true if your clubhead is coming from inside to outside the target line. The ball will start to the right and either go straight, curve to the right or curve to the left depending on your clubface position.

Technical research tells us that *clubface position* has the greatest effect on the initial starting direction of the ball. The ball will start approximately 70 percent in the direction the clubface is positioned. So if your clubhead is traveling straight down the target line and your clubface is open and aiming 10 degrees to the right at impact, the ball will start on a line about seven degrees to the right of the target. That information becomes particularly important when you intentionally try to hook or slice a shot. For practical purposes, you need only to be aware of the general relationship between path and face position.

The slower your clubhead is traveling and the more loft it has, factors that usually go hand-in-hand, the less curvature you will get on your shots. That's why you can curve your driver a great deal but can't get much hook or slice with your pitching wedge.

Squareness of contact has a big influence on distance and also can affect the curvature of a shot. If you don't strike the ball squarely with the center of the clubface, you will lose distance. You also will lose accuracy. Contacting the ball toward the toe end of the club will cause it to hook or curve right to left. Hitting toward the heel will produce a slice or left-to-right curve. Feeling where these off-center hits occur and knowing what they cause can help you analyze why the ball is doing what it is.

Angle of approach is the angle or steepness of your clubhead path, relative to the ground, as you swing into the ball. That combined with *dynamic loft*, which depends on both the angle at which the clubface is being swung into the ball and the position of that face relative to the ground at impact, determines trajectory, the up-and-down curve on which the ball travels.

Your angle of approach depends to a great extent on

your setup and ball position at address, so we'll go into greater detail on how it affects your shots in those chapters.

Clubhead speed, in combination with square contact,

Trajectory is the up-and-down curve of your shot, determined by angle of approach and dynamic loft. Your trajectory with a driver will be relatively flat and gets higher as the loft of the club increases.

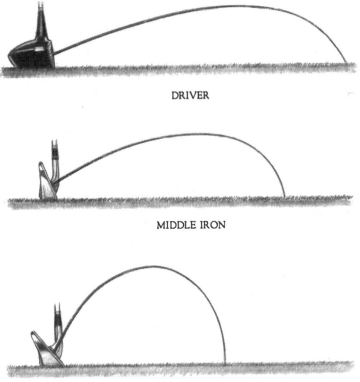

DRIVER

MIDDLE IRON

SHORT IRON

determines distance. The greater your clubhead speed, provided you strike the ball solidly and your path and face position are correct, the farther the ball will go. Even here, clubhead speed is dependent on a setup that will promote a *free swinging* of the arms and the proper movement of the body.

Every aspect of your ball flight is related to pre-shot fundamentals, which is why we have taken the time to acquaint you with these laws. If you know why the ball is flying as it does, you can go back to those fundamentals and correct any errors that crop up.

Let's look at some of the things that can go wrong if your fundamentals are faulty. For example, if your body and club are aimed to the right of your target and you make a good swing, the ball is going to travel to the right. You don't want that to happen, so you soon will do something to bring the ball back to the target. And chances are you will have changed your good swing into a bad one.

By the same token, if your setup or aim keeps changing from shot to shot, you probably will change your swing accordingly. After awhile your shot pattern will be so inconsistent that you will have no idea where the ball is going. You will begin to compensate for an improper setup by overworking your shoulders or hands, or both, which will cost you distance as well as direction and consistency. You will alter the rhythm of your swing, which will cost you clubhead speed and promote more off-center hits.

We have found that 90 percent of the students, at all

handicap levels, making their first visit to the Golf Digest Instructional Schools set up incorrectly. About 80 percent of them aim the clubface and/or the body to the right. So is this a common problem or what?

A good player aims the club in a specific direction and in a specific manner. The not-so-good player aims in a general direction, failing to position his body so he can make the proper swing motion on the correct path.

To play golf well, the solution is simply stated: *Aim the club down the target line and arrange your body so you can swing down that line.*

Simply stated, perhaps, but not so simply accomplished. In the remainder of this book we will offer concepts that will help you develop a working set of fundamentals. They will relate to such things as your desired ball flight, your body type, your swing requirements and even your personality. The five fundamentals we will discuss are the grip, the aiming of your club, your ball position, your posture or setup and alignment and, finally, your pre-shot routine. We will try to help you find your *own* fundamentals, tailored to your requirements and designed to help you swing the club in the most effective manner for *you*.

But we warn you that it won't be easy. You probably have read or heard that you must be natural and comfortable at address. Countless good players and teachers have said that. But that's a myth, because it doesn't happen in the beginning. And it's a myth that can be damaging to your ability to swing the golf club effectively.

The good player feels natural and comfortable with his grip and setup position because he has practiced those positions for a number of years. If your fundamentals are faulty, as is the case with most amateurs, you will feel uncomfortable while you are establishing the correct ones.

You should embrace this concept: A *contrived setup produces a natural swing and a natural setup produces a contrived swing.*

What feels natural to you at the moment may be wrong, so when you first get into the correct positions with your grip, posture and alignment, it undoubtedly will feel unnatural. We seldom put a student in the correct position without being told that it's uncomfortable. But you must accept that and work to learn the correct positions, reinforcing yourself with the thought that no matter how uncomfortable you feel at first, what you are doing is right and will pay off over the long haul. What feels contrived at the moment will give you a natural, free-flowing swing that will send the ball on-line to the target.

Eventually you *will* feel comfortable over the ball. But never get complacent. "Natural" can lead to "careless," and you must never be careless about the way you assume your grip and address the ball. You will need to work on your pre-shot fundamentals for the rest of your life—remember we said that's the first place the professionals look when they get into trouble with their swings. Once you have established the correct fundamentals and they are resulting in good shots, that's the first place you should look when problems arise.

2

HOW TO FIND
YOUR BEST GRIP

Holding the golf club correctly for your body type and swing may be the most important fundamental in golf. Your hands are your only connection with the golf club, so it stands to reason that they had better be placed on that club in the proper manner.

A sound grip allows the hands and arms to swing the club freely around your body on the correct path and insures that the hands can react to square the club at impact. Thus it affects the starting direction of the shot, the curvature, the trajectory and the distance—which happen to be all the elements there are in the flight of the ball.

To let all this happen, you must accommodate the position of your hands on the club to your physical structure, the way you swing and the way you want to play golf.

None of us is made the same. Hand size and grip strength vary. Consequently, there is no one grip that is

A correct grip allows you to swing the club freely and square the clubface at impact.

right for everybody. The ideal grip is one that allows the hands to work best together as a unit, one not dominating the other. When they do that, you create less friction between the parts of the swing and can achieve that goal of a free swing with the clubface squaring at the right time. So you create more clubhead speed with control But that ideal grip can vary from individual to individual depending on his or her physique, swing tendencies and desired shot pattern.

The *model* grip is one that puts the hands in what we

call a *position of neutrality*. This neutral grip is one in which the back of the left hand and the palm of the right face approximately down a line parallel to the target line. To visualize it, place your hands together with your fingers extended in a praying position. Lower them to an approximate address position and slide the right hand down until the curves of the thumb pads fit together, the left thumb fitting snugly between the pads on the right hand. The back of the left hand and the palm of the right should be facing each other and looking down that line parallel to the target. When you put your hands on the club in this manner, your grip should look much the same.

Whether you use the neutral grip or other variations that we'll discuss later in this chapter, it's important that the hands be positioned *as close together as possible* so they can work as a unit.

Let's look at some options you have in assuming the correct hold on the club. First, you can hold the club either more in your fingers or more in the palms of your hands. Holding it more in the fingers gives your hands and wrists more flexibility to cock and uncock and produce more clubhead speed and greater distance. But it gives you less control over the clubface. Holding the club more in the palms provides greater stability and control but less of that flexibility that produces speed and distance. To find out what is best for you, determine whether your greatest need is clubhead speed and more distance or better control over the clubface.

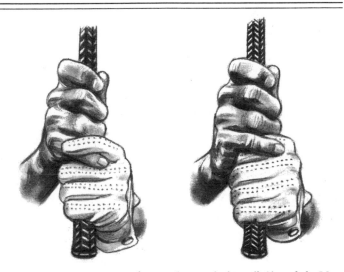

The two most common grip styles are the interlocking (left) and the Vardon or overlapping (right).

There are two basic styles of grips—the interlocking and the overlapping, or Vardon, grip. There also is a third style, the "unlap" or full-fingered grip that might be desirable for certain types of players and which we'll discuss later.

With the interlocking grip, the little finger of the right hand is interlocked or entwined with the forefinger of the left. With the overlap or Vardon grip, the right little finger is hooked around the left forefinger, laid between the forefinger and middle finger of the left hand.

There is no evidence that either the interlocking or the overlapping grip works better. The majority of good players use the overlap grip. However, Jack Nicklaus and Tom Kite, to name two, use the interlock, so it obviously can work pretty well. Jack's and Tom's fingers are shorter than normal, which is why they use that style. So the criteria you should use in deciding which is best for you are the size of your hands, the thickness and length of your fingers and the thickness of your palms. Experiment with both, if you wish, to see which puts the hands as close together and as unified as possible and best accommodates the swing you want to make.

Regardless of your method, the same fundamentals are used in finding your correct grip position. As you go through the steps we are about to outline, remember that they are only guidelines and that you may have to make the alterations we discuss later to fit your individual needs.

Before we get into the details, you must understand that you should not change the normal relationship of your shoulder, elbow, wrist and hand when you assume your hold on the club. Stand erect and relaxed, letting your arms hang at your sides. In 90 percent of the golfers we see, the hands will be turned slightly inward. This is essentially the position in which you want them when they are holding a club. This allows normal flexibility and rotation, a good wristcock and freedom of motion. Disturbing this normal configuration can tend to restrict your natural rotation and create too much tension in your arms and joints. Again, the particular mandates of your physical makeup and swing needs may indicate a change one way or the other.

To assume the model grip, take a club and place your

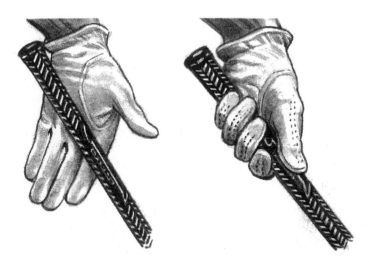

In the model or neutral grip, the club runs diagonally from the base joint of the left forefinger and rests underneath the heel pad of the left hand (left). The fingers are closed inward, around and up on the handle, with the left thumb resting just to the right side (right).

The neutral grip has the back of the left hand facing generally in the direction of the target (left). Closing the fingers inward around the handle of the club keeps that position basically intact.

left hand against it, fingers extended. The club should run diagonally from the base joint of your forefinger across the palm, resting *underneath* the heel pad of the hand. Now turn the fingers toward the palm, closing them inward, around and up on the handle of the club. When you do that, the back of the hand will change position only slightly and your thumb will end up resting on the right side of the club, just past center. If instead you turn the palm toward the fingers, your hand will be positioned too much on top of the handle.

By placing the club at the base of the fingers and in the palm and closing your fingers toward the palm, you insure a more secure grip that will stabilize the left hand and wrist and give you more control over the clubface when you swing. This is especially true when you want to hit the ball hard. As we said before, if you have the club too much in the fingers or let the handle ride up over the heel pad, or both, you create a concave wrist position that can cause excessive hand rotation and loss of clubface control. Because the left hand is your master hand in the golf swing, you want it firmly in control of the club.

To position the right hand correctly, place it against the side of the shaft, the handle resting across the roots of the fingers, snugly against the callous pads. Again, the first three fingers close around and upward, toward the palm.

If you choose to use the interlocking grip, the little finger of the right hand will hook under the forefinger of the left, resting between the forefinger and the index fin-

Left: Here's how the fingers should be placed, especially the "triggered" position of the right thumb and forefinger. Right: In the Vardon grip, the little finger of the right hand overlaps the forefinger of the left and the right thumb rests slightly to the left side of the handle.

ger. If you are using the Vardon or overlap grip, the right little finger hooks around the left forefinger, resting in the groove between that and the left index finger. How the little finger hooks around the forefinger in this style is important. If it sits too much on top of the forefinger, it sets the right hand too high or toward the left. If the little finger is snuggled too much into the groove, the right hand tends to be too far under or to the right. Either variation can cause trouble.

A word here about the "long" or "short" left thumb. It can rest on the club either in a short or arched position or it can be extended into a long position by sliding it down the handle. This extension should not be so severe that you feel constricted or uncomfortable. The long thumb provides greater wrist stability throughout the swing, but it also can restrict your ability to cock your wrists. We prefer a more neutral position in which the thumb is not arched but is laid comfortably along the shaft so you get more stability without restriction.

In any event, the left thumb fits snugly into the channel between the heel and thumb pads of the right hand. The right thumb falls naturally to the left side of the handle, forming a V with the right forefinger, which should be set in a slightly triggered position rather than

The "short" left thumb, placed in an arched position on the handle of the club (left), restricts the cocking of the wrists during the swing. So does the "long" thumb, one that is stretched excessively down the handle. A position in which the thumb is laid comfortably down the handle is preferred.

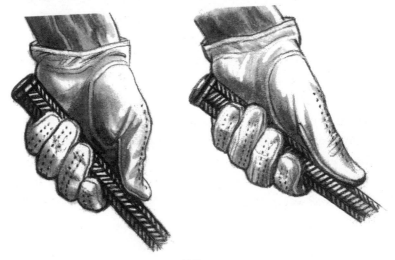

wrapped underneath the handle. Be sure not to pinch the closed end of the V too tightly together, because that creates tension where you don't want it.

If your hands are placed correctly together on the club, the palm of your right hand should be facing approximately toward the target and should be pretty much aligned with the back of the left. The Vs formed by the thumb and forefinger of each hand should point to a spot somewhere between your right shoulder and chin.

We emphasize that this model or neutral grip may not fit your particular needs, so you may want to make some adjustments to find the grip position that best fits your body and swing shape to give you maximum control over the clubface.

If you are of average height or taller, with reasonable strength and a swing that is relatively upright, and you have no problem creating enough hand speed to release and square the club through impact, you probably should use a grip that comes close to the model. However, if you are shorter and swing the club more around your body, you might want to turn your hands a little more to the right to accommodate that swing shape.

If you lack strength and need more hand action to create clubhead speed, you might want to place the club a little deeper in the fingers of your left hand, at the same time putting the left hand a little more on top and the right hand more to the right or under to facilitate the wrist hinge that will give you that hand action. Be sure that the

The ten-finger or unlap grip, in which all the fingers and both thumbs are on the handle, may be best for players who lack strength and need more hand action for clubhead speed.

palms are still facing. This also may be a solution if you lack flexibility in your wrists.

If you lack strength and have very small hands, you might consider the full-finger or unlap grip. We particularly see many women who, because of the strength factor or hand size, can't play effectively with the interlocking or overlapping grip.

The unlap grip is formed exactly the same as the other two, except that the little finger of the right hand is placed on the club rather than hooking around or interlocking with the forefinger of the left. With all eight fingers and the two thumbs on the club, the right hand is lower on the shaft in a more dominant position. This makes it easier to release and square the clubface through impact and recock the hands after impact, which in turn creates the needed hand and clubhead speed.

Experiment with this if the other grip styles aren't working for you. And let's hasten to add that the full-finger grip isn't necessarily limited to weak players. Bob Rosburg won a PGA Championship and Art Wall won the Masters using this very method.

Whatever grip style you use, it is extremely important to put your hands on the club with precision. You must match the bottom of the club with the shaft angle and the position of your hands to make sure that your fingers and hands remain in proper alignment with the clubface during the swing.

What you are looking for is the grip position that best keeps the clubface square as you swing back and through, releasing and squaring up in the impact zone. The best measure of your grip's effectiveness is always the way the ball flies—where it starts, how and how much your ball curves and how much distance you are getting.

If your hands are set too much to the left, your left hand too much under and your right too much on top of the club in the so-called "weak" position, the outside muscles of the arm are activated on the backswing and the wrist is prevented from cocking properly. This makes the first move on the backswing usually to the outside of the target line. From there the clubhead can move too quickly to the inside and get "laid off" with the face too shut. This in turn causes a reaction that forces the club to the outside

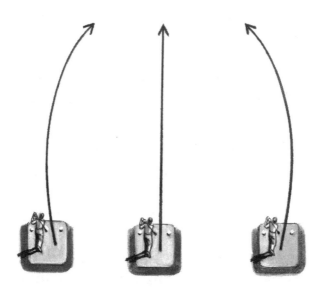

As a general rule, a "weak" grip can cause the ball to slice, a "neutral" grip will result in a straight shot and a "strong" grip can result in a hook.

of the target line on the forward swing, resulting in a pull, pull-hook or pull-slice, depending on what you do with your hands. Or you might get a shot that starts weakly to the right and tails off even more in that direction. Whatever variety you get, you won't like it very much.

If your hands are positioned too much to the right, the left hand too much on top and the right hand too much under, you will have a tendency to turn the clubface over too much through impact, causing shots that start to the right and hook too much to the left or that start left and hook even farther left.

In either case, when you see this happening, adjust your hands more toward the neutral position. That will help you hit your straightest and best shots.

If you are going to make a mistake, it is better to have your hands set too far to the right. The more the right hand sets under, the more it relaxes and softens the right arm, causing it to fold inward and get out of the way during the backswing. This hand position drops the right side underneath the left and promotes taking the club straight back, inside and up.

In fact, we have noticed a trend on Tour toward stronger grips, turned more to the right. Fred Couples, Paul Azinger and Bernhard Langer are three good examples. As long as this matches your swing type and doesn't produce excess curvature in your shots, it's probably the best way to go.

Almost every good player starts out with his hands in the left hand over/right hand under position because it's a more natural way to hold the club. Almost every motion we make in propelling an object forward—throwing a football or baseball, swinging a bat or a golf club—is performed with the right hand coming from under to over. Eventually, as a player starts to hook the ball too much with this strong position, he adjusts in the direction of the model grip. This lessens the rotation of the hands and lets him stabilize his left hand and wrist to keep the club from turning over too quickly through impact. This produces shots with less curvature.

So the model grip—or something approaching it—is best if you have the strength and talent to swing on the correct plane for your body and generate enough arm and hand speed to produce solid contact and generate sufficient distance. The model grip promotes good aim and alignment, encourages swinging the club on the proper plane and helps stabilize the hands and wrists against excessive rotation. This results in a simpler swing and more clubface control.

But, to repeat, if your physical structure, your talent level and/or the time you have to devote to the game preclude your using the model, you may have to make one or more of the accommodations we have suggested. This does not mean you never will be able to play good golf. Rather, it can help you play much better golf than you ever thought possible....and play it longer.

So experiment with your grip positions until you find the ones that work best for you. Your shots will let you know when you find the right combination.

Your *grip pressure*, which means applying pressure with your hands and fingers in the correct places and in the correct amounts, is at least as important as the position of your hands....maybe more so.

First, where should the pressure be? Basically, it should be applied with the last three fingers of each hand. This includes the little finger of the right hand, even though it may be off the shaft if you are using the interlocking or overlapping grip. Applying pressure with the last three fingers activates the muscles in the inside, or underneath, portion of your forearms, and these are the muscles you want to use during the forward swing.

Pressure in the last three fingers, rather than in the thumbs and forefingers, also reduces unwanted tension and allows the arms to swing more freely. That's because those inside muscles basically are attached at the elbows and most of them run no farther up the arm. Muscles activated by the thumb and forefinger, however, run all the way to the shoulder. So you can grip relatively firmly with the last three fingers and still leave the upper arms and shoulders free to perform without tension. Gripping tightly with the

To activate the proper muscles used in the swing and still leave the upper arms and shoulders free of tension, you should grip more firmly with the last three fingers of each hand.

thumbs and forefingers stiffens the muscles all the way up and restricts your swing and shoulder turn.

So the back three fingers are the grippers and the thumbs and forefingers are the feelers, giving you the touch you need in your swing. This is especially true of the right hand. The common tendency is to exert pressure with the right thumb and forefinger, and when this happens the right arm is forced high and toward the outside by the outside muscles of the arm. Then you take the club back to the outside of the target line and create the problems we discussed earlier. Also, because the right hand is lower on the club and closer to the clubhead, exerting too much pressure with the thumb and forefinger makes it more likely you will throw the club out of position.

If you are going to control the golf swing with your left hand and side, which we would prefer, you must exert more pressure with your left hand than your right (reverse these directions, of course, if you are a left-handed golfer). Controlling with the left hand helps keep the right hand from taking over during the critical change of direction at the top of the swing.

There must be *some* pressure with the right hand, of course. The right thumb and forefinger provide a cradle that supports the club at the top of the swing. And by applying pressure where the butt or heel pad of the right hand presses against the thumb pad of the left, you unify the hands, wrists and arms during the swing. That also tends to keep the elbows closer together and closer to the body, where you want them. So right hand pressure, especially in the middle two fingers, is important, but it should not be as strong as with the left.

How much pressure? The rule is simple: *Apply only as much pressure as you need to control the force of the club throughout the swing.*

This is why you see a flowing motion and continuity of rhythm in the swings of good players. But almost every player below the level of professional or top amateur grips the club too tightly. So we urge you to grip the club as *lightly* as you can, much lighter than you ever imagined, while still maintaining your ability to control the club.

A light grip frees your muscles for a relaxed but swift swing. The lighter your grip pressure, the more relaxed your arms are and the easier and faster they swing. You always can move a relaxed muscle faster than one that is rigid.

A light grip also allows you to feel the force of the club, and until you can feel that force you cannot make the golf swing perform the way you want. A lighter grip rids your arms and upper body of tension and your swing becomes freer, longer and more rhythmic.

How do you determine the lightest possible grip pressure that can still let you control the club and be effective for you? Individual strength and the length and weight of your club are factors here. You might want to experiment with different clubs. Or do some exercises to increase your strength. But the only sure way to find out how light your grip pressure can be is to hit practice shots, starting with as little pressure as possible and gradually increasing it until you can control the club while maintaining an arm swing that is free of tension.

Don't confuse *light* with *loose*. Your grip must be firm and solid so there is no slippage during the swing. The key to maintaining a solid and light grip at the same time is keeping your grip pressure as constant as possible throughout the swing. This gives you a more constant arm flow and more sensitivity for the force of the club swinging back and through.

If your grip pressure changes abruptly during the swing, you will change your arm swing, disrupt your rhythm and pace and alter your path and clubface position. This is especially true if you increase the pressure in your right thumb and forefinger, which is what usually happens.

This doesn't mean that your grip pressure won't increase throughout the swing. But in the good player it increases minimally and gradually in the left hand, from 10 percent or so of his potential grip pressure at address to still less than half at impact. The poorer player will grip too tightly during address and takeaway, with the left hand grip pressure slackening through impact. This means that at this point the right hand has taken over and is controlling the swing.

The amount of your grip pressure at address and through the swing will differ, of course, for different clubs and different shots. If you are going to swing a club longer and faster, you must hold onto it more firmly. Your grip pressure for a full driver shot will be greater than for a half swing with a wedge. That in turn will be greater than for a putt.

This difference is something that cannot be taught. You'll have to learn it for yourself. Start with a putter on the practice green. You'll find that when you are putting your best, your grip pressure remains light and constant. Move to the chip shot, and your pressure will be a little firmer, but still constant and tension-free. Move back to the pitch shot and eventually through all the clubs. As the club and proposed swing gets longer, your grip pressure will be increasing slightly at address. But it will remain within the range of a light grip that keeps you free of tension and allows the free arm flow you need to achieve the best feel for the swing.

DRILLS

Keep a Coin On Your Thumb

To insure that your hands stay unified throughout the swing, grip the club with your left hand, then place a coin on top of your left thumb, between the two joints. Fit the thumb pad of the right hand over the coin as you assume your right-hand grip. Then keep the coin in place as you swing. If it drops out, your hands are coming apart and your swing will lose some effectiveness.

Practice With the Claw

Take your normal grip, then slide your right forefinger over the top of the shaft and curl it under your right thumb. The shaft now will rest between the forefinger and middle finger. This drill will help eliminate pressure with the right thumb and forefinger, preventing you from casting the club at the top. It also prevents letting go with the left hand at the top of the swing and makes the hands work better as a unit. You may feel you don't have much control with the right hand, but don't compensate by overusing the right shoulder. Also, be sure to have some bandages on hand—the skin between your fingers may get raw after a few shots.

Take Right Hand Off After Impact

Make a normal swing and just let your right hand slip off the club *after* impact. Take a couple of practice swings, then hit four or five balls—on the first, let the right hand come off at the follow-through position, then let it slip off a little sooner each time until it comes off just after impact.

This drill gives you feeling for controlling the club with your left hand, confirming that you need more grip pressure in your left hand than your right. It also promotes a sense of your left arm pacing your right. It helps develop left arm speed and extension through the ball. It helps keep right arm and hand tension out of the swing. As a by-product, it will improve your takeaway. By realizing how much you are going to need your left arm on the forward swing, you will subconsciously start to use your left hand and arm more on the backswing.

Remember, let the right hand slip off *after* impact. Letting it come off *at* impact or before can do you more harm than good. Another potential pitfall is that you may think you need to apply more effort in your swing, but you really don't. Also, players who use the interlocking grip should do this drill with an overlapping grip or they will lose their grip pressure in the last three fingers of the left hand.

Keep Grip Pressure Constant and Light

Practice making a full swing while keeping your grip pressure light and constant throughout. This promotes proper pace and is an extremely effective way of slowing down your swing. It gives you a more constant rate of acceleration rather than a jerky action coming forward. Remember, the feeling is light, not loose. Don't get tight with your arms and loose with your hands.

Don't Ground the Club

Don't sole your club on the ground at address. Use just enough grip pressure to hold the clubhead slightly above the turf. This gives you the feeling of the light but firm grip pressure you need to control whatever club you have in your hand. It eliminates any downward pressure on the shaft at address and promotes a slower, smoother take-away.

3

HOW TO AIM YOUR CLUBFACE

Aiming the clubface properly sets up an instinctive reaction in your golf swing and in the release of your hands, arms and the clubface as it swings through the ball in the impact area. Proper aim makes you *want* to swing the club on line and allows an uninhibited squaring of the clubface to get the ball started on line.

In other words, striking your ball to the target is a lot easier if your clubface is pointing to that target at address. Clubface position influences almost everything else in the setup and swing.

For example, if you fear a slice, you might close the clubface at address to guard against it, and that's inviting disaster. You probably will promote a swing that will take the clubface outside the target line and bring it back across the ball to the inside. That can result in one of those shots that goes anywhere, either a pull or a banana-ball slice or some other aber-

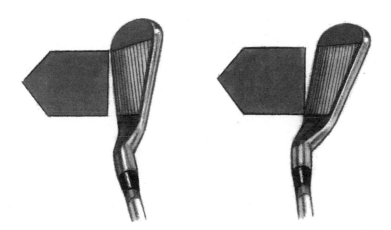

A closed face at address (left) can promote an outside-in swing that produces a pulled shot or a pull-slice. A slightly open face encourages a more inside swing path and promotes more release and speed in your swing.

ration that ends up nowhere near your intended target.

That's the worst-case scenario. On a more positive note, if you need a little more release in your swing, you might consider opening the clubface slightly at address. At the same time, close your stance ever so slightly, pulling the right foot a bit away from the target line. This encourages a swing path that goes back more to the inside and comes through from the inside, promoting more release and more speed in your swing. That helps you develop a slight right-to-left draw and hit the ball farther. We see a lot of good players who do this, and it might work for you.

The point is, you can adjust your aim to your swing

preferences and needs. You will have to experiment to find out what those are. Aim the club down the line on which you want the ball to start. The best beginning is to aim the club directly at the target and swing down that line. After that, adjust according to your swing tendencies.

Let's go back to one of our grip precepts—make sure your hands are placed on the club in proper position and *in proper relation to the clubface.* When your hands are in this position, the clubface should be aiming directly down the target line.

If you are having trouble identifying what your club-face should look like when aimed correctly, try this exercise. Fill in the scoring lines on an iron club with a black, soft-tipped pen. Take a white two-by-four board, lay it on the ground parallel to your target line and draw a black line on it at right angles to the target line. Then, as you

To identify a square club-face, align the blackened scoring lines of the face with a line drawn perpendicular to the target on a two-by-four board.

address your ball, make the black lines on your clubface line up with the line on the board. You'll know the face is square, and this will let you identify what it is supposed to look like when it is aimed on target.

To help you find that target and aim the clubface properly, we advocate using an "intermediate target". This shorter target might be a leaf, a divot, a clump of grass or some other identifiable spot from four to 12 feet in front of your ball that is directly on line between the ball and the target. The reason for the intermediate target is that it's easier to aim at a spot close to you than at a target 100, 150 or 200 yards away.

Just as it's extremely important to know how a correctly aimed clubface should look, it's important to perceive the target line with your eyes, tracking from the ball down that line through the intermediate target to the real target and back again. As you move into your address position, rotate your head and eyes down the line and back as you first fit the club behind the ball so it is aimed correctly, then fitting your body to the club. That's important! Aim the club first, then align your body to match the clubface. It's a point we'll pursue further in Chapter 5.

Let's amend the statement we made in the last paragraph—it's important to perceive the target line *correctly* with your eyes. How you see determines how you aim and subsequently how you swing the club. Correct use of the eyes is one of the least understood and most violated principles of good aim and alignment. Faulty optical alignment

Track your eyes down the target line by rotating your head, not lifting it.

is a major contributor to poor play among most golfers.

The most common fault is to cock the chin at such an angle that the eye line is set to the right of the target. We don't see many players who set their eye lines left, although it does happen. Whichever direction your eyes are looking, it is going to influence the way you position your clubface as well as your path and the compensations you must make with your hands and shoulders during the swing.

So to aim and swing the club on the line on which you want the ball to start, your eyes must be sighting down that line, which means your eye line must be parallel to the line.

To accomplish this, first *be sure your head is straight as you address the ball.* Don't tilt your head to one side or the other. Imagine a vertical line that runs directly in front of you and align your head with it. Practice in front of a mirror so you can see that your head is straight and you get the feeling of it being set that way.

Next, as you complete your setup, rotate your head slightly to the right, making sure your chin stays behind

Be sure your head is straight as you address the ball by imagining a vertical line in front of you and align your head with it.

your forehead. And when you look at the target, always do so by rotating your head to the left and then back to the ball rather than by lifting your head up and around.

Just before you start your backswing, *rotate your chin slightly more to the right or counterclockwise*, keeping your head and eyes properly aligned. As you do so, fix your left eye on the ball and keep it there throughout the backswing and forward swing through impact. This movement can be seen in the swings of almost all the great players. It rotates your head along the swing path and helps you get a better feel for that path as you take the club away and return it to the ball, promoting a sense of the inward and downward path your left arm and club should take from the top of the swing into impact.

Guard against the tendency to change your eye alignment forward or backward, right or left, especially just before you start your forward swing. *Keep your eye line constant throughout the backswing and through the impact area.* Soon after impact your head and eyes will rotate to the left to follow the flight of the ball.

Practice this by starting on the putting green, where your head and eyes will simply rotate because the ball is still on the ground. For shots that get airborne, your eyes will react to that flight and your head will come up naturally at the finish of the swing.

Your eyes conceive and your body receives the message. Developing proper eye alignment and head movement is a big step toward aiming and swinging in the right direction. And that means your shots will go where you want them to go.

DRILLS

Bandages for Your Eye Line

If you don't mind looking a little strange, this exercise will help you develop the ability to rotate your eyes properly down the target line. Take your glasses, if you wear them, or a pair of sunglasses and place two strips of tape horizontally on each lens, top and bottom and parallel to each other, so you have a slit in the middle to see through. Make sure the strips on each lens are lined up with those on the other lens. Now, because your field of vision is nar-

rowed, you will have to rotate your head and eyes properly when you look at the target and then back to the ball. This will help you identify the feeling of correct rotation. Next, put your body and eyes in position and make a golf swing, concentrating on holding the correct relationship of your eyes to the ball.

Use a Ribbon to Visualize

Stake a ribbon from about three feet in back of your ball and run it several yards out toward your target. Tee a ball in the middle of the ribbon. Aim your club down the ribbon and align your body to the ribbon. Sight your target by rotating your head and tracking your eyes forward along the ribbon. Next, rotate your head and track your eyes all the way to the back of the ribbon, then rotate and track them forward again until you can just see the golf ball. Then swing and strike the ball. This drill helps you visualize your target and the direction in which you want the ball to go. It also induces proper body and eye alignment and encourages the proper swing path back and through.

4

HOW TO FIND YOUR CORRECT BALL POSITION

Just as there is not one swing for all players, there is not one ball position that will work for everybody. We should say there is not one *set of ball positions*, because each individual should change the position of his ball at address to accommodate the club in his hand and the shot he has in mind.

The purpose in learning to position your ball correctly is to accurately locate it in relation to the bottom of your swing arc. This lets you bring the club into the ball at the proper angle and on the correct path and to square the clubface at impact with your hands and arms.

First you must understand *angle of approach* with the various clubs. As we said in Chapter One, this is the angle or steepness of your clubhead path, relative to the ground, as you swing into the ball. The club's angle of approach, along with its effective loft at impact, determine trajectory, the up-and-down curve on which the ball travels.

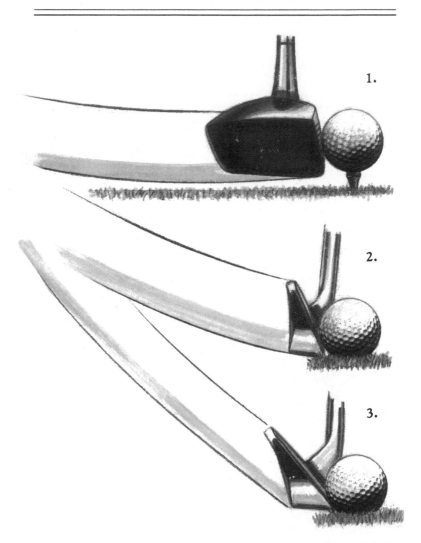

The angle of approach to the ball varies with the club—level to ascending with the driver and the ball on the tee (1), more downward with middle irons (2) and steeper yet with the short irons (3).

Without getting into scientific detail, and assuming you are fitted with a shaft that will return your club to the proper position at impact, let's look at the possibilities as they realistically affect your ball flight.

With a driver, when the ball is sitting off the ground on a tee, it is possible to swing into impact from above, level with or below the ball. If you contact the ball with the clubhead traveling on the horizontal or level with the ground and with the face square, and if you make center-face contact, the ball will fly on a normal trajectory.

If your club is approaching the ball at a steeper angle, from above horizontal, you will be striking the ball more obliquely. The ball may actually be launched at a lower angle than before because your club is coming in on a downward path, but the downward, more oblique angle produces more spin, and more spin produces a higher flight. The force behind the blow will be less and this shot will tend to "upshoot". It eventually will travel on a higher trajectory and probably won't go as far.

Conversely, if you have reached the bottom of your swing arc and the club is traveling upward at impact, the ball may actually start a little higher. But it will have less spin, and because of that will tend to fly on a flatter or lower trajectory and may, especially if you're into the wind or if the ground is firm, go farther than the other types.

That destroys the myth that you should tee the ball back in your stance if you want to hit a low drive into the wind. Instead, move the ball forward in your stance and catch it on the upswing.

The practicalities change a bit for a fairway wood or an iron shot, because your ball now is sitting on the ground. Usually you will not be able to swing up on the ball without topping it, because the ground will have got in the way. So your angle of attack must be either on the level or from above. The exception is when your ball is sitting up in rough or fluffy grass or when it's on a tee on a par-3 hole. It's often good to apply these principles in such situations.

On the usual fairway shot, you will get basically the same results with the same kind of swing as you would with a driver. A steeper swing, especially from outside to in, as a steeper swing usually is, will give you a high slice or a low pull or pull-hook, depending on your clubface position. A shallower angle of approach along the target line or from the inside will produce a more normal trajectory.

But to hit the ball *lower* from the fairway, you *do* position the ball back in your stance. This produces a steeper angle of attack, to be sure, but it also *delofts* your clubface. The ball will be launched at a much lower angle—how much lower depends on how far back in your stance you addressed the ball—and will never rise as high as a normal shot.

The opposite is called for when you need to hit a shot *higher,* as when you must get 5-iron distance but have to carry a tall tree. In this case, address the ball *forward* in your stance as far as possible, to the point where the clubhead is striking the ball exactly at or a fraction past the bottom of its arc. Then you will be getting as much dynamic loft as possible out of the club. Be careful not to position the ball too far forward or you will not strike it solidly and may even top it.

Achieving the correct angle of approach and effective loft for the shot required is a function of both ball position and setup position. We will address setup position in Chapter Five. For now let's examine only how you can position the ball properly.

To repeat, with a fairway wood or an iron—anytime the ball is sitting on the turf—you want to make contact with a slightly descending blow. With a driver and the ball on a tee, you ideally want to catch the ball after the club has passed the bottom of its arc and is slightly on the upswing. At the very least you want your clubhead coming in on the level.

Given those parameters, your ball position becomes an individual matter, dictated basically by your ability to strike the ball with the clubhead coming from inside the target line and the clubface square at impact. *The more difficulty you have returning the club from inside the target line, the farther back you should position the ball.*

In locating your correct ball position, we suggest that you don't align it strictly in relation to your feet but instead consider it in relation to your sternum or the placket on your shirt. Further, no matter what the position of your

feet, whether they be open or closed to the target, be sure
that the ball's relationship to your sternum is at right angles to the target line. This assures you of being able to position the ball consistently for the different clubs.

As a caveat, we feel that almost every amateur golfer
should play the ball more toward the center of the stance.
Playing the ball forward is a luxury that usually can be afford-
ed only by the good player with a strong leg drive, the ability
to shift his weight from the ground up and move his lower

*The position of the ball relative to your stance also varies with the club and
the intended shot—in the center or slightly to the right of center for the
short iron (1); slightly forward of center with the 5-iron (2);...*

1.

2.

body laterally so he can still strike the ball from the inside.

Most amateurs cannot move that well with their legs, especially if they are heavy-set or have lost some suppleness because of age or infirmity. Experiment to find the best position for your particular swing and physical capabilities, but use the center of your stance as a guideline.

For example, you want a very descending angle with the short irons to produce more spin, so the ball should be positioned in the center of the stance, maybe slightly to

...an inch or two farther forward but still well inside your left heel with the fairway woods (3); a couple of inches inside your left heel to just off the heel, depending on the strength of your weight shift, for the driver (4).

3.   4.

the right of center. Locating the ball in relation to your sternum will give you the feeling that your eyes are looking about at the top of the ball.

With a 5-iron, you want an angle that is not quite so steep, so the ball should be located slightly more forward. Feel that your sternum is set just at the back of the ball. Now you should feel you are looking more at the back of the ball than the top. This position encourages a slightly shallower angle and a path that still comes from the inside.

As you go to a fairway wood, you must dramatically change the angle of approach. The ball is still on the ground, but you want to sweep it or clip it off the grass, so you must move the ball even farther forward, maybe an inch or two. The ball will be well inside your left heel, but it should be far enough forward to encourage a shallower swing that will bring the clubhead into the ball on virtually a level path.

With a driver the situation changes even more dramatically. Now the ball is sitting on a tee and, ideally, you want to strike it with an upward blow. As we said, the really good player with a strong weight shift might play the ball off the inside of the left heel. But for most other players it should be positioned a couple of inches inside the left heel. Again, relate this position to your sternum and not your feet, because that will help you locate the ball more consistently.

This position at or near the left heel will change the angle at which you look at the ball, so that you will see

A tall player may have to position the ball farther forward in his stance (1). A player of average size should keep the center of his stance as a reference point (2). A shorter player who swings more around the body may need to play the ball farther back (3).

considerably more of the back of the ball. That will encourage you to strike it with the upward blow you want.

Your body type will be a major influence on your ball position. If you are tall—say, 6'2" or more—your swing probably will be a little more upright or vertical. So your ball position might have to be farther forward than normal to accommodate that swing shape. If you are of average height, you probably should consider the center of your stance, directly in line with your sternum, as the reference point when the ball is on the ground. A shorter player who swings more around his body probably should play the ball relatively farther back for all shots.

The key is that you must strike each shot with the club coming from inside the target line and the clubface squaring at impact. If you can't do that, if you are pulling or pull-slicing your shots, move the ball back in your stance until your shots start on line or slightly to the right. If they begin starting too far to the right, move the ball forward a little.

Experiment on the practice tee to find your correct ball position for the various clubs, then be disciplined enough to follow those findings on the course.

Don't get careless. Don't take ball position for granted, because it dramatically affects your swing and your ball flight. The good news is that this is something you can take care of before the swing begins. If you do, it will make that swing a lot more effective.

5

HOW TO SET UP FOR SUCCESS

Most bad shots are caused before the club is swung. As improbable as that sounds, it's true. We said in Chapter One that more than 90 percent of the amateurs we see prepare improperly to strike a shot. They either misaim the club-face, misalign the body or stand poorly to the ball. Unless you just happen to get lucky, improper preparation always leads to poor results.

How, then, do we set up for a successful shot? The process involves aiming the club and correctly positioning the ball, which we've covered in the two preceding chapters. After that, good setup incorporates correct posture and correctly aligning the parts of the body in relation to your target and projected swing path.

Let's first examine *posture*, the position of your body as you stand to the ball. Your posture, combined with alignment and aim, dictates how you will swing the golf club. So it's logical that you assume a posture that will help you swing the way you *want* to. If you *have* to swing a certain way to accommodate bad posture, which is almost always the case, the results are never going to be as good. Since the golf swing is an athletic movement—of the highest order, we might add—you must be in an athletically ready position to make that swing. That means you are light on your feet, your hands are sensitive to the club, your body parts are in position to move freely and your mind is free to react to your target and make the swing that will send the ball to that target.

We believe the swing should be controlled by the arms rather than the shoulders. The shoulders cannot swing. They turn and tilt as a result of the arms swinging. So the simplest and most efficient method of striking a golf ball is with a free arm swing that takes the club straight back, inside, around your body and up, then returns it from slightly inside the backswing path to along the target line and back inside it on the follow-through. So our posture precepts are based on promoting this free swinging of the arms. Those precepts are:

1. The weight usually should be set more on the right side than the left.
When we were kids learning golf, we were told to stand to the ball with our weight on the left foot. That myth is still around in some circles, even though there is no logic in it. It is not a natural position. If you stand with your weight

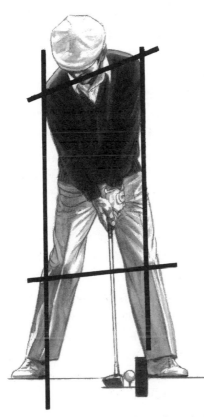

With the longer clubs, and especially with the driver, your weight should be more to the right side at address. With your right hand and right shoulder lower, this will happen automatically if you let it.

balanced between your feet, bend forward from the hips, put your hands together in a praying position, let your arms hang, then slide your right hand a few inches lower than the left, your weight automatically goes to the right side. That's exactly what happens when you address a golf ball with a club in your hand.

Further, it doesn't make sense to start with the weight on the left leg to support a movement that's going to the right on the backswing. It's much simpler to put the weight on the right leg so it can support the backswing from the very beginning. You eliminate an extra move.

Setting the weight right frees up the left side and allows you, in effect, to swing the left side around the right leg on the backswing, putting the left leg in position to move on the forward swing and the right leg in position to react and move forward into the shot. This is what we see in the swings of good players.

Setting up on the left side tends to put the swing in control of the shoulders, which creates tension and can cause a reverse tilt toward the target at the top of the swing. With the weight more to the right at address, you can swing your arms with enough motion to pull them behind the ball, where you want them, on the backswing.

The weight should be set more to the right for almost every full, normal shot. At the most, the percentage should be about 60-40 to the right side, and the ratio changes with the club. Remember, we told you that the all-important angle of approach depends not only on your ball position but on your setup position as well. The more your weight is to the right, the shallower your swing arc will be, travelling parallel to the ground longer through the impact area. The more the weight goes toward the left, the steeper your arc and angle of approach will be.

A good rule of thumb for the ball on a tee or for a normal lie in the fairway is that *the farther you want to hit the ball, the more your weight should be on the right side at ad-*

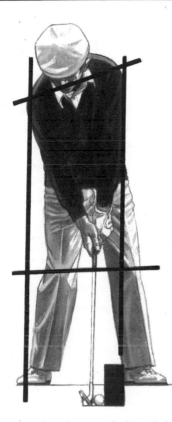

From the 5-iron down through the shorter irons the weight can be more balanced, but there should never be more on the left except for special shots.

dress. As the shot and the club in your hand gets shorter, your weight should be set more toward the left. With the short irons and up to about the 5-iron, balancing the weight 50-50 is perfectly acceptable, probably preferable. But we don't believe there ever should be more weight on the left side than the right, except for special situations. If you need to play a shot especially low, set the ball back in your stance and put your weight more to the left to get a steeper angle of approach and a delofted club. And there are certain short shots around the green that require setting the weight left. Other than that, don't lean in that direction.

Your weight placement is pretty much dictated by the position of your head and sternum in relation to the ball. The farther back you set your head to the right, the more your body tilts to the right and the more your weight falls that way. If your head and sternum are directly over a ball that is centered in your stance, your weight will be pretty well balanced.

It's important to remember that while more weight may be on the right side, that weight should be set to the inside of the right foot. Your weight should not move too far toward the outside of the right knee and foot during the backswing. We don't want you to stifle your motion, body turn and weight shift going back, but overdoing it can create a breakdown in your right leg, which is the foundation of your backswing.

2. The weight should be toward the balls of the feet.
Recall other sports you have played or watched that require motion. We can't think of any in which the players start from their heels. Almost every athlete who needs motion starts from the balls of his feet. The runner runs on the balls of his feet. The basketball player guards his man from the balls of his feet. The football player starts from the balls of his feet. So does the discus thrower and the shot putter.

Golf, too, requires good leg movement. Addressing the ball with your weight toward the balls of your feet promotes a feeling of catlike mobility, a lightness in your feet and a readiness to shift and turn that will promote the good leg movement that is the foundation of a free swing.

Notice we didn't say put the weight on your toes, or even on the balls alone. If you set your weight too far forward you'll topple over. The weight should be between the heels and the balls of your feet, but more toward the balls. Then you're ready to make an athletic movement.

3. The knees should be flexed just slightly in most cases.
As a guideline, your knees should be flexed only enough to unlock them, no more than three or four inches in most cases. This might not hold true for everyone, especially taller players like George Archer who might need more knee flex so they can get set properly to the ball. This is particularly true of a taller person with long legs and short arms. But too much flex in the knees is a common fault that can throw the weight too much toward the heels and create a weak support in the right leg as the player swings around it.

However much you flex your knees, the keys are to tilt your upper body properly, which will happen as a reaction to looking downward at the ball, and to keep your weight toward the balls of your feet. This will promote a feeling of springy tension in the insides of your legs and

At address your knees should be slightly flexed, your weight toward the balls of your feet and your upper body tilted forward from the hips to promote a catlike feeling of lightness and readiness to turn and shift during the swing.

the backs of your thighs. Letting your weight go too far back toward the heels forces your back into a position that is too erect. It places more pressure on your spine, creates more tension in your back and inhibits your ability to turn and shift properly.

So flex your knees, tilt your upper body and set your weight to induce that catlike feeling, ready to spring into action.

4. The back should be straight but tilted forward from the hips so that the arms hang freely from the shoulders.
Keep your spine straight by creating a slight tension in the small of the back, sticking out your buttocks slightly. But don't mistake *straight* for *erect*. Tilt your straight back forward from your hips, giving you the feeling that you are "out over the ball," probably much more than you are used to. And don't let your head slump. To find this position, start by standing with your back and head erect, eyes looking straight ahead. Then tilt your upper body forward, keeping your head and neck in the same position relative to your spine. If your head slumps, your optical alignment will be distorted and your chin will tend to get in the way during your swing.

While keeping your spine straight as you tilt forward, allow your shoulders to relax and slump and hang naturally. This in turn will let your arms hang freely suspended. There is a common misconception that the arms and hands must be in a straight line with the clubshaft at address. This causes players to arch their wrists and get their hands high, locking the wrists, tightening the arms and promoting a shoulder-oriented swing that is too flat. Instead, the arms should just hang, with the hands always inside the eye line. The left arm will hang straight and you will feel there is plenty of room under your left armpit, giv-

ing you freedom to swing the arm away from your body.
The right arm will be slightly folded and tucked closer to
your right side. The line along the left arm, wrist and hand
should appear relaxed and hanging fairly straight down.
The hands and wrists should not be arched, and *there will
be a definite angle between your arms and the clubshaft.*
Check yourself in a mirror to make sure of this.

The angle of your arm hang will vary, of course, depending on the length of the club you have in your hands. With a
pitching wedge they will hang pretty much straight down.
With a driver your arms will appear to be reaching a bit more.

1.

*Your arms should hang
freely from the shoulders,
your hands always inside
your eye line. The angle
of your arm hang will
vary with the club...*

But, if you sole each club properly, the length of the club will determine this and you won't have to worry about it.

The correct combination of body tilt and arm suspension promotes a full, free arm swing and a more upright swing plane, which we feel is most effective.

From this "over the ball" position you may feel that you are going to topple forward, especially if you have had your weight too much on your heels and have been yanking the club too quickly to the inside on the backswing, which in turn has been forcing you to swing out over the ball with your upper body on the forward swing to get back

...reaching more with a driver (1), less with a 5-iron (2) and hanging almost straight down with a wedge (3).

2.   3.

on the proper path. But stick with it. You'll soon get accustomed to the correct posture and will find you no longer have to make any compensating moves.

5. The right side should be set lower than the left, the knees cocked toward the target.
This happens naturally, simply because your right hand is lower on the club than your left. Your right shoulder will be lower than your left and your entire right side should feel "broken", soft and passive. The upper body will be set behind or to the right of the lower body. All of this allows the right side to turn easily out of the way on the backswing, making it easier for the left side to turn around the right.

To enhance this feeling, cock your knees targetward or to the left as you address the ball. The right knee should be set forward of the right toe, or more toward the target. Be sure to do this on a line parallel to the target line. Don't twist your lower body open or to the left of that line when you cock your knees.

Practice assuming this position in front of a mirror and note that your body will be in somewhat of a "K" position, your right eye approximately over your right knee. This position will vary a little with the club you are using, but you should always be in the basic K.

Cocking your knees to the target also makes the right leg a firmer support for the backswing, letting you better control the hip and shoulder turn and the arm swing going back. It frees up the left knee, giving it more time to build

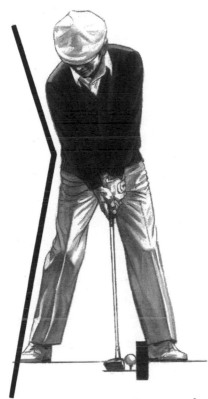

Your right side should be set lower than your left, which happens naturally when you put your right hand on the club lower than the left, and your knees should be cocked to the target in a reverse "K" position.

momentum as it turns in toward your right thigh on the backswing and allowing it to move forward more easily on the forward swing.

The *width of your stance* is important, but it's an individual thing that depends on your physical stature and flexibility. The rule of thumb is that *your stance should be as wide as possible to give you a stable foundation but not so wide that it inhibits a free arm swing and body turn.*

That's why a thinner, more flexible player can use a relatively wide stance that allows him to make a faster, more aggressive swing. He is flexible enough that the wide stance doesn't restrict him. A player who is larger, perhaps stockier with less flexibility, must play from a narrower stance to be able to make a free arm swing.

To find your optimum stance width, start with a driver and a stance that is as wide as the outsides of your shoulders, measured from the insides of your heels. Make several swings and gradually widen your stance until you feel you are restricting your hip turn and you can't swing your arms fast enough to generate sufficient clubhead speed. That stance is too wide. Now gradually narrow your stance until you feel that your swing is getting too loose and sloppy with too much turn. Again, you can't swing your arms fast enough because you will tend to lose your balance. Now you're too narrow.

Do the same with all the clubs in your bag. You'll discover there's an optimum width for the distance you get out of a shot and that there's a point of diminishing returns on both ends. Within those parameters, work back to the middle to find the best width for you with each club.

In general, your stance will become progressively narrower as you go from the driver down to the wedge, because your swing need not be as full and aggressive with the shorter clubs.

The wider stance promotes a harder, more aggressive swing. A narrow stance allows a free arm swing but makes you swing slower and more "within yourself" to keep from losing your balance. And that's not all bad. So we would recommend that if you are going to err, do so on the side of narrow.

The best posture in the world doesn't do you much good if you don't *align your body* properly. This is the final step in setting up to prepare yourself for a good shot.

We discussed aiming your clubface in Chapter Three. Now we'll talk about aiming your body to accommodate the aim of that clubface.

That simply means, as a standard, aligning all the parts of your body on a line parallel to the target line or the line on which you want the ball to start. To do this we like to *use the six lines of alignment*. These six lines start with the target line and include lines drawn parallel to that target line that run through the toes, knees, hips, shoulders and eyes.

Imagine that you have five boards and that you place one against each of those areas of your anatomy. If you are aligned correctly, each board will run parallel to the target line and you will be in a position that allows your arms to swing freely down the correct path and strike the ball to the target.

Simple enough. The problem is that too many players feel that the body should be aimed at the target. That's a

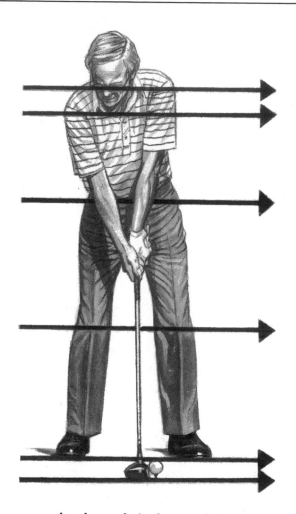

To insure you are aligned correctly for the normal shot, use the "six lines of alignment." Start with the target line and imagine five other lines that run across your toes, knees, hips, shoulders and eyes, all parallel to the target line. This aligns all parts of your body as you want them.

mistake. Aiming the body at the target automatically aims the clubface to the right of the target. That, along with faulty optics, is probably the reason so many golfers aim to the right.

Look at it this way. If your body alignment is square

When your clubface is aiming at the target, your body must be aligned "parallel" left of that target. This creates the feeling of being set up far left of the target, how far depending on the distance. Don't be uncomfortable with this. Trust that it is correct.

to the correctly aimed clubface and if it is parallel to the target line, it cannot be aimed at the target. If you could see yourself from a down-the-line view, you would see that your body is set to the left of the ball and is aligned to the left of the target. Your body must be set *parallel left*, parallel to your target line but aimed left of the target.

This creates the feeling of aiming far to the left of the target. This feeling is exaggerated by an optical illusion created by distance. Many players, if they are at all aware of the parallel left concept, make the mistake of assuming that because their shoulders are about two feet from the ball at address they should have their bodies aimed at a spot two feet left of the distant target. This still will get them aimed to the right of the target.

Because of that optical illusion, you must feel you are set a great deal farther left than the relationship of your body and the target line at address. A general guideline is that at 100 yards your shoulders will appear to be aiming eight yards left of your target. At 170 yards they will seem to be set 12 yards left and at 240 yards 16 yards left. Individual perceptions may vary because of posture and visual peculiarities, but if you understand the concept you can experiment to find what is right for you.

Remember the statement we made in Chapter Three. Aim the clubface *first*, then align your body parts perpendicular to that clubface. Then you will be set parallel left. Accept that in your mind and swing with the trust that the ball will go to the target.

The square or parallel alignment we have described is the standard. We would encourage you to use that as your basic position, but there are some variations you should consider and experiment with.

With the driver, you may wish to drop your right foot slightly farther from the target line into a bit of a closed stance. This encourages an easier rotation of your right hip on the backswing. It promotes a backswing that is a little more around your body and helps you deliver the club back to the ball more from the inside and on the shallower angle that you want.

Depending on your flexibility, you also may want to set your left toe more perpendicular to the target line and adjust your right toe to the right or clockwise to further encourage the turning of the right side going back.

With a short iron, on the other hand, you may want to pull the left foot slightly back from the target line, which sets your body in more of an open position. This restricts the length of your backswing and makes your arc slightly more vertical to accommodate the length of the shaft and produce the steeper arc you want.

Experiment with these variations, keeping in mind that you always need to make your hands, wrists and the clubface compatible with your swing path to get the ball to go to the target.

As you can see, there is not just one setup and one alignment that works. There are different body types and there are different clubs. Posture, setup and align-

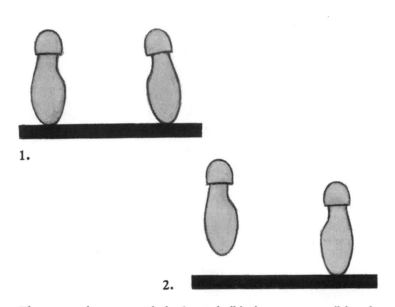

The square alignment, with the feet and all body parts set parallel to the target line (1), should be your standard, but you may want to vary for certain shots. With the driver you may want to set your stance more closed, the right foot farther away from the target line (2)....

ment must be adapted to each club. Work with all of them to determine what works best for you with each of them.

But always remember that a consistent posture, aim and alignment that get your mind and body reacting to the target lead to repeatable golf swings and a ball flight that will send your shots where you want them to go.

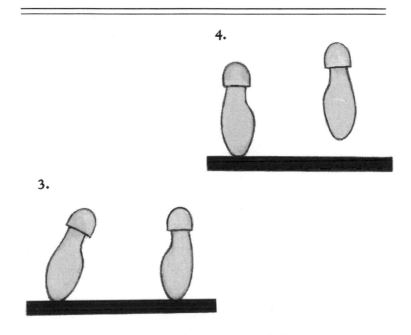

...*You may want to square the left foot and angle the right foot more to the right (3) to encourage an easier turn away from the ball. With a short iron, you may want a more open stance (4), the left foot away from the target line, to restrict your backswing and create a more vertical arc.*

DRILLS

Use Clubs for Alignment

Place two clubs on the ground parallel to your target line, one a couple of inches outside the ball and the other next to your stance line. Then set up and swing. This is an aid to creating proper alignment, making sure your feet and your other body parts are aligned parallel to the target line.

You also can use this device to determine how far parallel left you should feel you are set. Place the clubs on the ground like this either at a marked practice area or at spots on your course where you know the distances to your target are accurate. Put one club on the target line and the other underneath your shoulder line at address. Stand just behind the shoulder-line pointer club and sight down it. Note the spot in the target area where the club is pointing. That's the spot at which your shoulders should be aiming, with the rest of your body aligned accordingly. When you set up properly, you should barely see your left shoulder as you rotate your head and eyes toward the target. If you see too much of your left shoulder, you are aligned too far to the right.

(For left-handers, the whole procedure should be reversed. Your concept is that you want to be aiming *parallel right*.)

6

ROUTINE GETS IT ALL STARTED

The problem almost every golfer has, at one time or another, is getting from the static positions we have described in the preceding chapters to the swing itself.

That's not hard to do when you're making a practice swing without a ball in front of you. It's really not too hard when you're hitting balls on the practice tee under no pressure and you can rake over another ball if you miss a shot. Where it gets very hard to do is on the golf course, where every shot counts and there are no second chances.

Obviously you want to make your swing on the course resemble your practice swing as closely as possible. To do this, you have to forget about mechanics and think only about where you want the ball to go. This is done through visualizing your target and how the ball will fly to it, a process we discussed thoroughly in Volume One of this series.

Next you have to find a way to trigger your swing, getting it started without letting mechanical thoughts intrude on your mental picture of the target. You do this by establishing a consistent pre-shot *routine*, a simple yet ideal way to tie together your pre-swing fundamentals and your in-swing motion. This routine is done in a certain time span that lets you approach the ball, address the ball, waggle the club and start your swing in the same manner each time.

This does a couple of wonderful things for you. It eliminates that awful moment of takeaway, a time of dread for most players who start their swings from a static position. Because they fear that time when they must move the club back, the continuity and flow of the swing is disrupted right from the start. With an established routine, that moment becomes no different than any other moment in the course of setting up to and swinging through the ball. The swing starts reflexively without the player having to worry about it.

A good routine also gives your body a sense of timing, a feeling for the rhythm and sequence of motion, a feeling of alertness and fluidity that puts you in a relaxed state at the start of the swing. Once you develop such a routine, your body won't know whether it's the first shot of a practice session or the last shot of a tournament. It will react the same in either case.

Your routine, of course, involves all the things you must do before you take the club back—place your hands

Keep your individual routine consistent on all shots. Pick out your target and intermediate target from behind the ball (1). Place your hands on the club and step into position with your right foot as you set the club (2)....

on the club, aim the clubface down the target line, align your body to the clubface and the target line and position your body to the ball in the proper posture.

The mechanics of your routine are quite simple. You can do it any way you want, but here are our suggested guidelines, based on how we see most good players do it:

Always keep in mind that you should think *forward* to start the swing back. Eye the ball, then the target, then the ball...and swing.

Start from a few paces behind the ball, looking

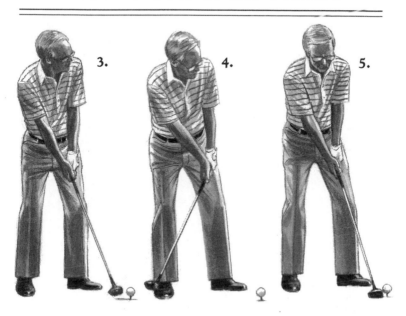

...Adjust your stance and body and rotate your head and eyes down the target line (3). Waggle the club a time or two as you glance at the target (4). Rotate your eyes back to the ball, make your forward press and go (5).

through the ball down the path to the target. At this point you should be visualizing the target and how you want the ball to get there, and you should never lose this shot picture throughout your routine and swing. By now you should have a plan for your swing, a key or two that will direct you in making the swing that will send the ball where you want it. Make a preparatory swing down the target line to internalize the feel of the swing you want so you won't have to think about mechanics.

Pick out that intermediate target over which you

want the ball to start and, with the shot picture still clearly in mind and your body relaxed, place your hands on the club in the proper position and begin your approach to the ball. Walk to the ball and move into the address position at a right angle to the target line and slightly behind the ball, all the while keeping your eye on the intermediate spot.

Step forward with your right foot as you place the club behind the ball and aim it down the target line. Place your left foot in the correct spot related to the ball position you want, then adjust your right foot for the stance you want. Next set your knees, hips, shoulders and eye line the way you want them—all parallel to the target line for the normal shot—at the same time setting up in the correct posture. Glance at the target a time or two to reinforce its image and the aim of your club. Do this as you make your waggle or waggles. Then make your forward press and swing the club away.

The waggle and forward press are all-important. The waggle keeps you in motion and helps create a keen sense of feel for the shot at hand. If you waggle correctly, it previews the swing, activating the muscles you need for the swing you want to make.

The waggle should be made in a free and easy manner, using the last three fingers of the left hand, cocking the wrists without a lot of arm movement straight back from the ball and returning to the ball from the inside. Thus it gives you the sensation of a miniature swing. If you are going to make a full swing, especially with the driver, the waggle should be long and flowing. If you are preparing to play a little punch shot, it will be shorter and quicker. It should vary similarly for each type of shot you are going to play.

The number of waggles you make is up to you, but the longer you stand over the ball the fuzzier your target picture becomes, so we would suggest only two or three waggles, at the most.

The forward press activates the swing. There are many ways to do this, but we prefer a slight push of the right knee toward the left. This moves the left knee a bit toward the target, pushes the left hip slightly upward and relaxes and lowers the right side at the same time. This helps the right side turn more easily, promoting a free arm swing, and activates the feet and legs for their part in the swing.

Your routine, leading to and incorporating the takeaway, should never vary, and it should be done in a rhythmic sequence within a specific time span. This time span can vary with each individual. Do it at your own pace. Usually, the slower and more deliberately you do it, the smoother and more controlled your takeaway will be. But don't get too slow. A 10- to 15-second interval from first step to takeaway is within the correct range. If you take too much time, your target picture will fade, you will lose the feel of the pre-shot sequence and mechanical thoughts may begin to intrude. But whatever time span you allow yourself, try to make it constant and go through the same movements every time.

It's also vital to stay in motion during your routine. Keep your feet moving, even if it's just a slight up-and-down motion, as you refine your stance. At the same time, keep your hands and arms moving with your waggle. This establishes the muscular feel in your hands and feet that spreads to the rest of your muscles and prepares your body for the shot. The heartbeat of every golf swing is in the hands and arms and feet and legs. If you stop and get into a fixed position, the flow and continuity that triggers your swing is disrupted.

The routine is like every other element of pre-swing preparation and the swing itself. It needs to be practiced so you can develop trust in it. Practice it on the range and on the course. Especially practice it in your warm-up sessions before you play a real round. Force yourself to go through it the same way each time. At first you certainly will feel that you are hitting the shot before you are ready. But once you get through that stage you will find your body wanting to go instinctively at the right moment.

When that happens, you will be able to incorporate all your fundamentals into an effective swing, and you will have taken a big step toward better shots and better scores.

Bob Toski is considered by many to be golf's foremost teacher. One of the country's top players in the mid-1950s, he won the World Championship of Golf and was leading money winner on tour in 1954. He virtually retired from professional play at age 30 to devote his life to teaching.

Jim Flick is the Master Instructor of the Nicklaus/Flick Golf Schools. In more than 35 years of teaching golf, Flick has become recognized as one of the world's finest instructors and one of golf's most dedicated students.

Larry Dennis is a former senior editor of *Golf Digest*, where he headed the magazine's instruction program. Winner of national awards as a sports writer and editor, his books include *How to Play Consistent Golf* (with Tom Kite), *Golf Digest's Book of Drills* (with Jim McLean) and *How to Become a Complete Golfer* (with Bob Toski and Jim Flick).

Bob Toski, Jim Flick and Larry Dennis are the authors of Volume I of the Golf Digest Learning Library, *A Swing for a Lifetime*.